Baseball
In Indianapolis

MR. BASEBALL.
Indianapolis-born Owen J. "Donie" Bush spent 65 years in professional baseball as a player, manager, and owner in Indianapolis. He first played in Indianapolis in 1908. After his playing days, he returned to Indianapolis as a manager, from 1924 to 1926. Then he became the president and chief executive officer of the Indians in 1942 and headed the club until the late 1960s. The field his team played on was named in his honor late in his career. The Indians played at Bush Stadium until 1995. (Photo courtesy of Indiana State Museum.)

BASEBALL
IN INDIANAPOLIS

W.C. Madden

ARCADIA

Published by Arcadia Publishing,
an imprint of Tempus Publishing, Inc.
2 Cumberland Street
Charleston, SC 29401

Printed in Great Britain.

Library of Congress Catalog Card Number: 2002116265

For all general information contact Arcadia Publishing at:
Telephone 843-853-2070
Fax 843-853-0044
E-Mail sales@arcadiapublishing.com

For customer service and orders:
Toll-Free 1-888-313-2665

Visit us on the internet at http://www.arcadiapublishing.com

CONTENTS

Acknowledgments   6

Introduction   7

1.   Professional Baseball Comes to Indianapolis   9

2.   The Indianapolis Indians   25

3.   The Federal League   69

4.   Black Baseball   77

5.   Semi-Pro Baseball   89

6.   Youth Baseball   99

7.   Collegiate Baseball   105

8.   Players from Indianapolis   113

9.   Vintage Baseball   119

Bibliography   128

ACKNOWLEDGMENTS

I HAVE TO first thank the Society for American Baseball Research (SABR). I wouldn't likely have written this book if I had not been the president of the local chapter, because Arcadia contacted me looking for an author in the Indianapolis area. I suggested myself and that's how I got the opportunity to do this book. Several SABR members also helped me with this book, including Jay Sanford, who provided some of the early images of Indianapolis teams.

The Indianapolis Indians were, as always, a great help in providing information and photos about their team. Tim Harms combed his photo files and provided them. Also of great help was Brian Drake, the commissioner of the Men's Senior Baseball League in Indianapolis. And thanks to all the others who provided information, interviews, baseball cards, and photos for the book.

1887 INDIANAPOLIS HOOSIERS. John T. Brush purchased the St. Louis Maroons from the National League and moved the team to Indianapolis in 1887, calling the team the Hoosiers. The team continued to perform dismally on the field and ended up in last place. (Photo courtesy of Jay Sanford.)

INTRODUCTION

EXACTLY WHEN baseball came to Indianapolis is difficult to say. The first games were likely not published in any newspaper and could have been played before the Civil War. The first published accounts of organized games came soon after the Civil War. The Base Ball and Cricket Club of Indianapolis gathered for a picnic on August 11, 1866—a tin cup went to the poorest player on the team. Town ball was evident around the state as well that year, and two teams met at Camp Morton in Indianapolis in a "match" game for the state championship. A team from LaPorte beat the Westerns, an Indianapolis team, 49-21, in a marathon game that spanned four hours and fifteen minutes.

The following year, more and more baseball games found their way into print. The Star City Club of Lafayette and the Washington Nationals, the most famous amateur baseball club at the time, came to Indianapolis to take on two local clubs. The two teams battled in a July double-header at Camp Burnside. A crowd estimated at five thousand watched the Actives of Indianapolis beat Lafayette, 54-31, in a six-inning affair. Then the Washington team beat the Western Club of Indianapolis, 106-21, in nine innings in the afternoon affair. Later that month, the first evidence of Black baseball in the Circle City was published. The Eagles, a team of Negro workers from the Bates House hotel, played the Mohawks, a team composed of barbers. Baseball was beginning to become a favorite summertime sport in the capital.

The sport has progressed on an amateur and professional level ever since. Indianapolis was host to a major league franchise for a few years early on, and has settled for a minor league team since 1915. Talk of a major league franchise came about again in the 1980s with a proposed team called the Indianapolis Arrows, but that never materialized and the Indianapolis Indians continued as the only professional team in the Circle City.

Today, the sport is enjoyed by many throughout the city, whether they be fans or players.

INDIANAPOLIS LOGO. This was the first logo used by an Indianapolis team, in 1876. The Indianapolis Westerns were part of the International Association that year. The following year, the team changed its name to Blues. (Art courtesy of Randi Madden.)

ONE
Professional Baseball
Comes to Indianapolis

IN 1869, the undefeated Cincinnati Red Stockings, the first openly professional team, came to town wearing beards, short pants, and long red stockings. The undefeated professionals took on a team of local scrubs in a converted cornfield at the northeast corner of Delaware and South Streets. Indianapolis became another victim. The Red Stockings would win 57 games and tie one on their trip around the country. The two teams met again the following year in Cincinnati, and this time Indianapolis gave the unconquered Reds the thumping of their life. The scrub team was led by a battery made up of brothers Aquilla (pitcher) and Ben (catcher) Jones. The disappointed Red Stockings disbanded shortly thereafter.

The first professional team in the Circle City was formed in 1876 and was called the Indianapolis Westerns. The Westerns played their games at a park located at Delaware and South Streets. W.B. Pettit organized the team. The following year the nickname was changed to the Blues—a name that came from the color of their uniforms—and the team won the pennant in the International Association by beating every Canadian team they played. Their only loss was to a team from Hartford, Connecticut. The Blues were built around a battery of pitcher Eddie Nolan and catcher Frank "Silver" Flint, both of St. Louis. The pitcher became known as "The Only Nolan," because he was the only pitcher on the team. Nolan had a reputation for mowing down players with a curveball. Flint had the task of catching those curves with his bare hands as no mitts were used back then. The following season, the Blues moved to the League Alliance, considered by some to be the first minor league.

The Blues joined the National League in 1878. Indianapolis opened the season on May 1st in Chicago and lost 5-4 before 2,500 cranks (the term for fans back then). The Blues blew a 4-2 ninth inning lead. Nolan was tagged for the loss. He wasn't as proficient in the National League and finished the season with a 13-22 record. The team ended next to last with a 24-36 record. John Clapp managed the team, which lost $5,000. Clapp had nothing left to pay players, so the team broke up at the end of the season.

Pro baseball took a siesta in Indianapolis until 1883. Indianapolis fielded an independent team and compiled a respectable record of 95-47 against teams from the National League, American Association, and Northwest League. The Hoosiers beat teams like the New York Metropolitans and the Baltimore Orioles.

Then in 1884, Dan O'Leary reorganized the Indianapolis Hoosiers and joined the American Association (AA), considered a major league back then. The AA was also referred to as the "Beer Ball League" because it authorized (and encouraged) the sale of beer at the ballpark. The poor squad began the season losing its first three games to St. Louis and finished next to last with a 29-78 record. Jim Gifford and Bill Watkins were managers that year. Pitcher Larry McKeon led the league in losses with 41. League officials decided to oust the Indianapolis franchise from the league after the disappointing season.

The Hoosiers began the 1885 season with the Western League. Bill Watkins continued to manage the squad, and Phillip Igae became the secretary and treasurer of the league. The team played its first game on April 18 and lost to Milwaukee at Washington Park. The Hoosiers bounced back from the poor start and won the first half of the season with a 13-2-1 record. The second half opened suspiciously, with the league taking on the court over Sunday baseball. Blue laws in Indianapolis forced the club to play out of town at Bruce Park located at College Avenue and Twentieth Street. When league attendance dropped, several teams folded, but not the Indianapolis Hoosiers. A league meeting was held at the Indianapolis Grand Hotel to replace the departed teams, but financial considerations ended any speculation of replacements. The league disbanded. The final standings left the Hoosiers with a 27-4-1 record and an empty feeling. J.W. Keenan led the league in homers with three, while McKeon topped the league in wins with 11. O'Leary sold his superstars to Cincinnati for $10,000, an extraordinary price back then. He sold the rest of the team to Detroit, including farm boy "Big Sam" Thompson, who would later make his way to the National Baseball Hall of Fame in 1974.

The St. Louis franchise of the National League was purchased by John T. Brush and moved to Indianapolis in 1887. "Maroons" was changed to "Hoosiers." Brush was a real scrooge and proposed an A-to-E grading system for players with salaries ranging from $2,500 to $1,500. The team played at Athletic Park on the corner of Capitol Avenue and Sixteenth Street, which could be reached by mule car. Sunday games were played out of town at Tinker Street Park and Bruce Park to dodge the city law that prohibited games on the Sabbath.

The Hoosiers opened the season with a loss to the Detroit Wolverines on April 12. The team continued to perform dismally on the field with way too many errors. Like a revolving door, the team went through three managers—Watch Burnham, Fred Thomas and Horace Fogel—none of whom had a winning record. The Hoosiers ended up in last place with a 37-89 record. On October 20, the Hoosiers held an exhibition game against the Cuban Giants, a team of black players. About a thousand fans dared the cutting winds to witness the game, which was won by the Hoosiers, 13-8. The two teams met again the next day. The Hoosiers were leading 2-0 when the Cubans walked off the field in protest after a "bad" call by the umpire, Tug Arundel, who was a catcher for Indianapolis. "We want to win or lose games on their merits," said the Cuban manager. "This is the worst kind of farce."

Harry Spence took over as manager in 1888 and the team improved a little, finishing next to last with a 50-85 mark. Indianapolis changed managers again in 1889, but it didn't help. Frank Bancroft was replaced mid-season by Jack Glasscock, who finally pulled off a winning mark (34-32). Remarkably, the team had a pitcher with a winning record: Amos "The Hoosier Thunderbolt" Rusie went 12-10. He would go on to a great career and eventually be named to the Hall of Fame. The Hoosiers still ended up next to last.

The National Brotherhood of Baseball Players was formed in 1890 to improve salaries, so Brush withdrew his team from the National League rather than pay the players more money. Brush sold his players to the New York Nationals for $69,000. Indianapolis would not host another major league team until the Federal League was formed.

After a couple years without a pro team, Indianapolis sponsored a team called the Rainmakers in 1892 in the Western League. Rain was about the only thing the team could produce as fourteen games were washed out early in the season and the team began with eight losses before they posted a victory. The team finished dead last with a 15-39 record, a .278 winning percentage. That team as well as the league disbanded.

The Western League made a better comeback in 1894 when Ban Johnson, a sports editor for the Cincinnati Commercial-Gazette, reorganized the league. The Hoosiers were back in operation with Brush again as the owner. Brush also owned the Cincinnati Reds of the National League, so he began sending players to Indianapolis for more seasoning. The Hoosiers started off slowly until Brush began sending some major league players to Indianapolis, a move that irked President Johnson. The move didn't help the Hoosiers much as they finished the season in sixth place with a 60-64 record.

Before the 1895 season, the Hoosiers new manager, W.H. "Billy" Watkins, made a promise to do better. "Won't swear to it, but we are intending to put spikes on our shoes and climb for it," he explained in the *Sporting Life*. Watkins managed the 1895 Indianapolis team to a first-place finish and a 78-43 record. The next season opened on May 1 with a more determined owner and team. Indianapolis received lots of reinforcements from Cincinnati, including pitcher Bill Phillips and outfielder George Hogriever. Phillips finished the season with a 12-4 record, while Hogriever hit .402. Infielder Motz and outfielder Jack McCarthy led the league in hitting with .420 averages. Those performances helped the Hoosiers win the league championship with a 78-43 record. The league tried to prevent the "farming" of players, but Brush continued the habit, since it wasn't against any league rules.

The following season, the Hoosiers finished second to the Minneapolis Millers. The two teams met in a playoff series and Minneapolis beat Indianapolis four games to two. The 1897 season began with a bang with the Hoosiers, who began calling themselves Indians for the first time, shutting out the Grand Rapids Gold Bugs, 10-0. That began a winning streak that lasted three more games. Indianapolis continued to dominate the league the remainder of the season and easily won the pennant with a 98-37 mark. A trio of Indianapolis pitchers dominated the league. Jot Goar, who was purchased from the Pittsburgh team in the National League, led the league in ERA (1.30) on his way to a 28-8 record. Frank Foreman was 27-9 and Bill Phillips was 30-10. The Hoosiers faced Columbus in the post-season series and won three games to two. Each player received a $75 bonus.

The 1898 season got off to an uncertain start. Watkins left to manage Pittsburgh and he took a couple of key players with him. Bob Allen took the Indianapolis helm and the team started off the season with a 16-2 mark. The Hoosiers hung in there until August when they began to melt under the hot sun and finished second behind Kansas City. Phillips continued his winning ways with a 29-8 mark on the season. Some 90,000 fans saw the Hoosiers play that season at the Ohio Street Park.

Like a roller coaster ride, the Hoosiers were back up at the top of the hill the next season. After a sluggish start, Indianapolis began to get some momentum and won 12 straight in July. When the first-place Minneapolis Millers came to town late in the season, the Hoosiers won three of four games to take charge. Although the team won one game less than the Millers, they had three fewer losses and won the pennant by finishing a game up in the standings.

Johnson decided to rename the league American League and join the ranks of the major leagues. The Indianapolis franchise joined the American League for 1900, but it was still considered a minor league at that point. Watkins was fired from Pittsburgh, so he bought the remaining Indianapolis stock and became the team owner and manager. He decided to establish a new park on Washington Street near Rural. The team acquired some new players as well and got off to a fast start, holding on to first place until a series of injuries began to take their toll. The Hoosiers finished the season in third.

After the season, American League owners decided to reorganize and move more franchises into cities occupied by the National League to directly challenge it. Watkins decided to try and form the American Association to compete with the American League, but his attempts failed. Instead, he had to settle with joining the Western Association. He was able to keep those players reserved under contract; however, the rest of the players were moved with the franchise to Philadelphia to become the Athletics. The team got off to a good start, but attendance was poor and Watkins soon had to let players go, because he could no longer afford to pay them. He finally decided to sell the team to Matthews, Indiana. The poor team went from a 46-26 record to 56-78 and sixth place.

GEORGE "ORATOR" SHAFFER, OUTFIELDER, 1878. He was the best hitter on the squad with a .338 batting average. For the Philadelphia-born outfielder, it was one of his best seasons in his 13-year professional career. He ended his career as a .282 hitter. (Photo courtesy of Transcendental Graphics.)

FRANK T. BRUSH. Brush first became involved with baseball in Indianapolis when he purchased the St. Louis Maroons from the National League and moved the club to the Circle City in 1887. Later, when Indianapolis became a minor league team, Brush owned it and used it like a farm system for his club in Cincinnati. (Photo courtesy of the National Baseball Hall of Fame Library, Cooperstown, N.Y.)

WATCH BURNHAM, MANAGER, 1887. Burnham was the opening day manager for the club. After the team got off to a shaky 6-22 mark, he was fired and replaced by Fred Thomas, who didn't do much better. (Photo courtesy of Jay Sanford.)

"HANDSOME HENRY" BOYLE, PITCHER, 1887-89. Boyle recorded the most wins (13) on the season for the 1887 Indianapolis Hoosiers. He also had 24 losses, though. He pitched in 38 games, 37 of which were complete games. In those days, pitchers usually finished a game they started. He played six years in the majors in all. (Photo courtesy of Jay Sanford.)

13

JOHN "PEBBLY" GLASSCOCK, SHORTSTOP, 1887-89. Glasscock had a lengthy 17-year career in the majors. He took over as the player-manager for the Hoosiers in 1889 in mid-season. The team became a winner under his leadership the remainder of the season; however, the Hoosiers still ended with a losing mark. Glasscock helped his own cause as he had the second highest batting average (.352) in the league. He went on to 17 years in the majors. (Photo courtesy of Jay Sanford.)

EMMETT SEERY, OUTFIELDER, 1887-89. Seery roamed left field for the Hoosiers. He had some pop in his bat and was one of the leaders on the team in triples and home runs. In all, he played nine seasons in the majors. (Photo courtesy of Jay Sanford.)

PATSY CAHILL, OUTFIELDER, 1887. Cahill played in 68 games and batted a paltry .205. His meek performance led to his release from the team. (Photo courtesy of Jay Sanford.)

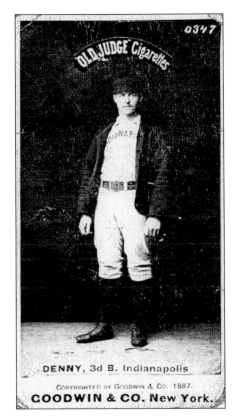

JERRY DENNY, THIRD BASEMAN, 1887-89. He led the team in batting average and was one of the league's home run leaders—12 in 1888 and 18 in 1889. He even pitched in one game. Denny played 13 years in the majors and finished with a .260 career batting average. (Photo courtesy of Jay Sanford.)

HOT LINER AT SHORT

GUARDING FIRST BASE

OLD SCORECARD. A scorecard from the 1884 season featured The Brooklyn Atlantics vs. the Indianapolis Hoosiers. Brooklyn finished in ninth that season, while Indianapolis finished eleventh. (Photo courtesy of Transcendental Graphics.)

OTTO SCHOMBERG, FIRST BASEMAN, 1887-88. He was the starting first baseman for the team in 1887 and hit a lofty .305, but the following season he was used as a substitute. He played for Pittsburgh in the American Association before coming to Indianapolis. (Photo courtesy of Jay Sanford.)

EGYPTIAN HEALY, PITCHER, 1887-88. John J. "Long John" Healy went by "Egyptian" as his playing name. The hurler had the distinction of leading the league in losses (29) in 1887. He didn't do much better the next season as he lost 24 games, while winning 12. He played eight seasons in the majors with a career mark of 79-136. (Photo courtesy of Jay Sanford.)

LARRY CORCORAN, PITCHER, 1887. The right-handed pitcher came to Indianapolis at the end of his eight-year career. By then he was spent. He lost two games with a 12.60 ERA before the team let him go. Ironically, his career started on a high note when he won 43 games in 1880. He finished with a 177-90 lifetime record. (Photo courtesy of Jay Sanford.)

GEORGE MYERS, CATCHER, 1887-89. Myers played for Buffalo and St. Louis before coming to the Hoosiers. He played 424 games in the majors and finished his career with a .203 batting average. (Photo courtesy of Jay Sanford.)

1889 INDIANAPOLIS HOOSIERS. The 1889 team was the last Indianapolis team to play in the National League. The team finished in next to last place with a 59-75 record. Amos "The Hoosier Thunderbolt" Rusie was on the team and in this photo. Others in the photo are Henry Boyle, Charlie Getzien, Charley Bassett, Dick Buckley, Jerry Denny, Jack Glasscock, Paul Hines, Jack McGeachy, Emmett Seery, and Marty Sullivan. (Photo courtesy of Jay Sanford.)

DICK BUCKLEY, CATCHER, 1888-89. Buckley shared the catching duties in 1888 with Con Daily and hit .273. He played eight years in the majors and posted a .245 career batting average. (Photo courtesy of Jay Sanford.)

LEV SHREVE, PITCHER, 1887-89. The right-hander came from Baltimore in 1887. After a 0-3 record with a 13.79 ERA in 1889, he was shown the door. Lifetime, he posted a 19-37 record. (Photo courtesy of Jay Sanford.)

JACK MCGEACHY, OUTFIELDER, 1887-89.
McGeachy spent half of his major league career with Indianapolis. He played center and right field for the Hoosiers. (Photo courtesy of Jay Sanford.)

"ACE" STEWART, SECOND BASEMAN, 1896-99. Asa Stewart came to Indianapolis from the Chicago Colts of the National League. He was named the team captain and helped the Hoosiers finish in second place his first year with the team. (Photo courtesy of Patrick Stewart.)

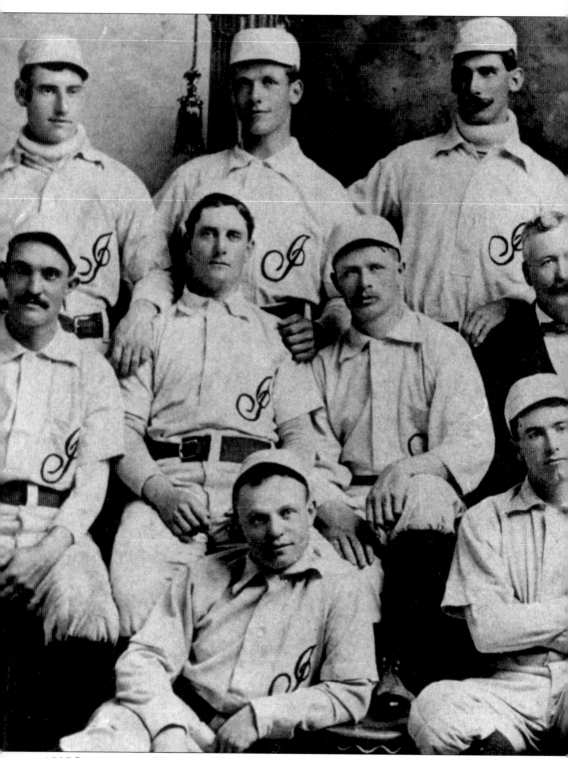

1897 INDIANAPOLIS HOOSIERS. The 1897 team won the championship of the Western League with this squad. Bill Watkins (center) managed the team to a first-place finish. William Gray

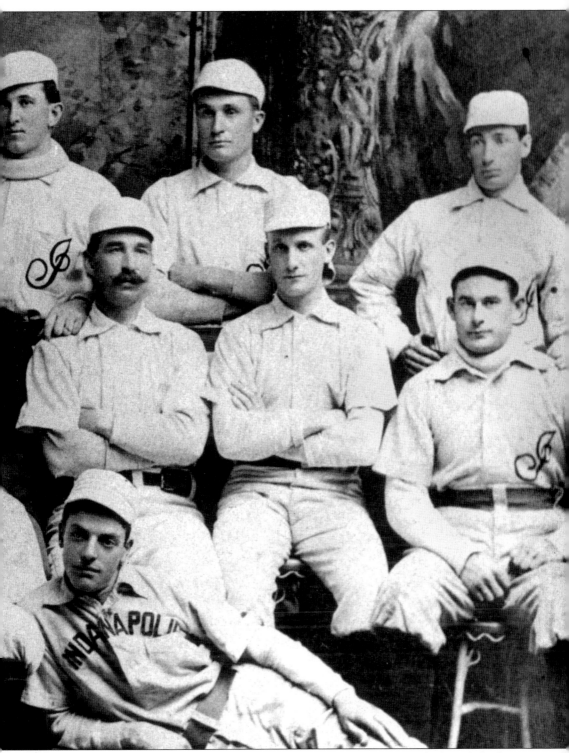

led the league in homers (19) and Francis Foreman had the most wins (30) and the best winning percentage (.769). (Photo courtesy of the National Baseball Library.)

Magnates of the Western League. The owners of the Western League in 1898 were, from left to right: (sitting) T.J. Loftus, Columbus; M.J. O'Brien; Ban Johnson, president; J.H. Manning, Kansas City; G.A. Vanderbeck, Detroit; and C.H. Saulpaugh, Minneapolis; (standing) Robert Allen, Indianapolis; M.R. Killiea, Milwaukee; Connie Mack, Milwaukee; Charles A. Comiskey, St. Paul; and G.H. Schmelz, Grand Rapids. Johnson went on to found the American League. (Photograph courtesy of the National Baseball Library.)

TWO

The Indianapolis Indians

INDIANAPOLIS FIRST used the nickname Indians in 1897, but the team went through a couple of other names-Hoosiers and Browns—before Indians became a permanent fixture in 1911. The ownership also bounced around in those early days until Jim Perry bought the team after the 1927 season from W.C. Smith, whose family had owned a portion of the club since 1914. Two years later, Perry died in a plane crash near Fort Benjamin Harrison and his brother, Norman, took over the team. Norman ran the family's Indianapolis Power and Light Company.

The Depression brought about hard times and after not bringing a pennant home for over a decade, Perry decided to sell the team in 1942 to Frank E. McKinney and Owen J. Bush, who first played for the team in 1908. The duo held onto the franchise until 1952 when they sold it to the Cleveland Indians. Cleveland lost a half a million dollars over the next four years and wanted to move the team. McKinney and Bush stepped forward again, and with the help of the Indianapolis Chamber of Commerce, led a public offering of the team with a capital stock of 16,000 shares at $10 per share. The public had less than a month to purchase the shares or the Indians would be history. The response by the public was overwhelming as $205,000—$45,000 more than the initial goal—was raised. The team was saved.

That public company, Indians, Inc., remains today with Max Schumacher as its chairman and president. After several years during the 1950s and '60s when the team was not financially successful, the team began a string of profitable years in 1973 that continues today. Starting in the 1980s, dividends and stock buybacks have been available for shareholders. In 2002, shareholders were offered an opportunity to sell their shares to the corporation for $9,200 per share.

Ironically, Cleveland provided a working agreement with Indianapolis for only one more season before making a switch after the 1956 campaign. Minor league teams began being directly affiliated with major league teams in the 1930s and Indianapolis joined the parade in 1939 with the Cincinnati Reds. In Indians history, the Reds have had Indianapolis as an affiliate on five different occasions, the last being 1993 to 1999. The Indians were twice aligned with the Chicago White Sox in the 1950s and 1960s. For nine seasons, from 1984 to 1992, the Indians were part of the Montreal Expos system. The Indians had short stints with the Boston Braves, Pittsburgh Pirates, Cleveland Indians, and Philadelphia Phillies. The Milwaukee Brewers replaced the Reds, and their agreement runs through 2004.

During the more than 100 years of existence, the Indians have had some great teams. The Indians became charter members of the minor league American Association in 1902, and Watkins led the team to the championship. George Hogriever scored 124 runs to lead the league, and Bill Fox stole the most bases (49). After dipping all the way to last place in 1905, the Indians won the title in 1908 behind a league-leading 28 wins by Rube Marquard, who would go on to the Hall of Fame. Marquard also struck out the most batters (250). After a decade of poor performances, the Indians returned to the top in 1917 with Jack Hendricks as manager. The Tribe then won the Junior World Series over Toronto.

Another 10 years passed before the Indians got to the top again in 1928 behind Bruno Betzel's leadership. Then the Indians won the Junior World Series over Rochester. Fred Haney, Rabbit Warstler, Adam Comorosky, Emil Yde, and Steve Swetonic were named to the All-Star Team.

Two decades passed before the Indians hit the top again. Al Lopez delivered the team to the championship in 1948 with 100 wins, yet the team lost in the playoffs. Ted Beard led the league in runs scored (131); Les Fleming knocked in a league leading 143 RBI; and Bob Malloy won 21 games to lead the league. Those players were named All-Stars as were Jack Cassini, Pete Castiglione, Earl Turner, and Jim Bagby, Jr. Fleming was also named the most valuable player. The following season, Lopez led the team to a second-place finish, but the Indians won the playoffs as well as the Junior World Series. Froilan "Nanny" Fernandez was named MVP. Pitcher Mel Queen was selected to the All-Star team.

Six years later, the Indians finished first, but lost the playoffs with Kerby Farrell at the helm. Rocky Colavito set a team record hammering out a league-leading 38 homers. Herb Score led the league in wins (22) and ERA (2.62), and set an American Association record with 330 strikeouts. Score was named MVP and Farrell was picked as the best manager. All-Stars also included Harry Malmberg, Hank Foiles, Owen Friend, and Sam Jones. Farrell brought home another pennant two years later in 1956. Indianapolis also won the Junior World Series over Rochester. Roger Maris was the star in Game Two of that series with two home runs and seven RBIs. Pitcher Stan Pitula tied for the lead in wins (15). Bill Harrell was the only player named to the All-Star team.

The early Sixties brought some great teams to Indianapolis. The Tribe won the pennant in 1961, but lost in the playoffs. Cliff Cook was named MVP, while manager Cot Deal was the top skipper. Don Pavletich, Claude Osteen, and Don Rudolph were named to the All-Star team. The '62 team was just as good with the same results, but with a different manager, Luke Appling. That squad included All-Stars Tom McCraw, Al Weis, Jim Koranda, and Frank Kreutzer. McCraw also led the league in batting average (.326), while Koranda had the most RBI (103). In 1963, the Indians switched to the International League and won the championship with Rollie Hemsley as the manager. Don Buford was the MVP and The Sporting News minor league player of the year after leading the league in batting average (.336), runs (114), hits (206), doubles (41) and stolen bases (42). Fritz Ackley won pitcher of the year honors in leading the league in wins (18) and ERA (2.76). Those two were named to the All-Star team as was Grover "Deacon" Jones. The following year, the Indians moved to the Pacific Coast League where they played five seasons before rejoining the American Association in 1969.

The Seventies also brought about some good teams. Vern Rapp led the Tribe to the Eastern Division title, but lost the playoffs in 1971 and 1974. The '71 All-Star team included Bill Plummer and Milt Wilcox. Rapp was named manager of the year. The Tribe All-Stars in '74 were Doug Flynn and Tom Spencer. Rapp was again the top manager. Then in 1978, Roy Majtyka managed a division winner as Champ Summers was named MVP and Sporting News minor league player of the year. Again, the Indians lost the playoffs. Besides Summers, the other All-Stars from the Tribe were Harry Spilman, Ron Oester, and Arturo DeFreites. Other future members of "The Big Red Machine" spent time in Indianapolis, including Pedro Borbon, Bernie Carbo, Dave Concepcion, Dan Driessen, George Foster, Ken Griffey, Ray Knight, and Hal McRae.

The Eighties marked the best decade in Indians baseball history. The 1982 team won the Eastern Division and the playoffs. George Scherger was manager of the year, while Tom Lawless and Gary Redus were All-Stars. The Tribe repeated the feat in 1986 with Joe Sparks as manager of the year. Casey Candaele was an All-Star that season. The biggest hit in Indians history came in 1986 in Game Seven of the playoffs against Denver. With the Indians trailing by one run and two out in the bottom of the ninth inning, Billy Moore delivered a sharp single to left off of Rob Dibble, driving in two runs for the championship. The following season the team finished in third place, but whipped the opposition in the playoffs for its second championship in a row. Sparks was again named the best manager in the league. That team had several all-stars as well: Jack Daugherty, Luis Rivera, Dallas Williams, and Pascual Perez. Indianapolis made it a three-peat when it won in 1988. Bob Sebra was named pitcher of the year. All-Stars included Johnny Paredes and Billy Moore. The Tribe made it a grand slam of championships the following season with Tom Runnells as manager. Mark Gardner was named pitcher of the year and the team had three other All-Stars: Junior Noboa, Jeff Huson, and Larry Walker. Other players who starred for the Tribe during the eighties included Delino DeShields, Andres Galarraga, Marquis Grissom, and Randy Johnson.

After a five-year drought, the Indians reeled in another championship in 1994 with Marc Bombard leading the team. Willie Greene, Doug Jennings, and Barry Lyons were named All-Stars that season. Bombard guided the team to another first-place finish the next season, but the team lost in the playoffs. The 1995 team made its mark with several home run records. The team set an all-time record for professional baseball with 13 grand slams during the season. The club also set the franchise record with 193 long balls. Greene led the team with 19 homers. Eric Owens was named MVP. All-Stars included Steve Gibralter and Drew Denson. Halfway through the 1996 season, the team closed Bush Stadium, its home since 1931, and moved downtown to Victory Field. Dave Miley directed the team into the playoffs. Eduardo Perez was the only All-Star on the team. In 1998, Triple-A baseball expanded to 30 teams and the Indians joined the International League.

The new century brought about a new affiliate, the Milwaukee Brewers, and a championship team. Steve Smith guided the Indians to the pennant in 2000. After winning two five-game series for the league title, the team went to Las Vegas and captured the Triple-A World Series. Closer Bob Scanlan was the team's MVP after recording a club-record 35 saves. Horacio Estrada led the circuit with 14 wins.

WASHINGTON STADIUM. The Indianapolis Indians called Washington Stadium home until Perry Stadium was built in 1931. The wooden park was first built in 1905 and the Indians played their first game there—an exhibition inner squad game—on April 1. Owner Norman Perry installed lights to Washington Stadium in 1930 and the Indians played their first night game on June 9. More than five thousand fans attended the game, which attracted some notables like Kenesaw Mountain Landis, the commissioner of Major League Baseball. The park was located near the site of the current Indianapolis Zoo. (Photo courtesy of the Indiana Historical Society.)

MONTE CROSS, INFIELDER, 1909. Cross came from Kansas City during the season and played 77 games for a dismal Tribe team which finished in sixth place. His batting average was dismal as well at .167. The shortstop with 15 years in the majors turned 40 years old while with the Indians. After the season ended, the Indians toured Cuba and compiled an 8-6 record.

CROSS, INDIANAPOLIS

HAYDEN, INDIANAPOLIS

JOHN HAYDEN, OUTFIELDER, 1908-10. Hayden, who played three years in the majors, came from Louisville in a trade in 1908. The Indians ended up getting the best deal as he won the league batting title that season with a .316 average, leading the Tribe to a pennant. He also led the league in hits (186), total bases (261), and triples (18). His performance led to him being drafted by the majors, but he returned to the Indians the next season. He led the team in triples in 1909 (9) and 1910 (10). And in 1910, he led the club again in hitting with a .278 average.

29

BURKE, INDIANAPOLIS

JIMMY BURKE, INFIELDER, 1909 AND 1911. "Sunset Jimmy" played seven years in the majors as a utility fielder before coming to the Indians in 1909. He hit .246 for an Indians team that finished in fourth place. He was also the leading base stealer with 27 swipes during the season. He played a short stretch as well in 1911.

RECORD CROWD. A record 22,163 fans came out to Perry Stadium to honor infielder Frank Sigafoos on July 19, 1933. The overflowing crowd was allowed to line the outfield walls and foul lines. (Photo courtesy of Indianapolis Indians.)

BUSH STADIUM. Hundreds of people wait to get in Bush Stadium during its final days. The park was the home of the Indianapolis Indians for more than 60 years. Norman Perry had the stadium built in 1931 and named it Perry Stadium in honor of his brother, who died in an airplane crash two years earlier. Perry Stadium cost $350,000 to build and hosted its first game on September 5, 1931, before a crowd of 5,942. After Perry sold the Indians, the field was renamed Victory Field during World War II in 1942. However, Perry retained ownership of the park until selling it to the city in 1967. Victory Field became Owen J. Bush Stadium in honor of the man who had been involved in Indianapolis baseball for more than 60 years. In 1995, the stadium was added to the National Register of Historic Places. The following year, the Indians left the park for a new field in downtown Indianapolis. Bush Stadium was used as an auto race track for a couple of years, but then became vacant.

AL LOPEZ, CATCHER AND MANAGER, 1948-50. Player-manager Lopez guided the Indians to the team's only 100-win season in its history. He also guided the Tribe to its longest winning streak (14 games) and second-best winning percentage (.649). Then Lopez went on to manage in the major leagues for 17 seasons. He recorded the eighth-best winning percentage in history. That led the National Hall of Fame to elect him in 1977. (Photo courtesy of Indianapolis Indians.)

HERB SCORE, PITCHER, 1952, '54, '62-63. The left-handed hurler fired the best single season record in Indians history when he went 22-5 in 1954. He also had the best ERA (2.62) and the most strikeouts in the league (330), which earned him MVP and Rookie of the Year honors. *The Sporting News* named him as the minor league MVP, too. He was promoted to the Cleveland Indians where he was the American League Rookie of the Year in 1955. He pitched in the majors for eight seasons before returning to Indianapolis again. He ranks third in career strikeouts with 530. (Photo courtesy of Indianapolis Indians.)

1956 INDIANS. The 1956 Indianapolis Indians won the American Association with a 92-62 record. The players were, from left to right: (front row) Stan Pawloski, Billy Harrell, Earl Averill, Rudy Regalado, Al Jones, Stan Pitula, manager Kerby Farrell, coach Johnny Hutchings, Stu Locklin, Larry Raines, Ed Gasque, Dolan Nichols, and Bud Daley; (back row) club house

boy Fred Schlegel, Ted Beard, Russ Nixon, Joe Altobelli, John Gray, Howie Rodemoyer, Rog Maris, George Spencer, Dick Tomansek, Murph Murszewski, Bobby Young, and trainer Mert Prophet. (Photo courtesy of Indianapolis Indians.)

LUKE APPLING, MANAGER, 1962. Appling guided the Tribe to a first-place finish in 1962. He was named manager of the year by the league and *The Sporting News.* Two years later he was named to the Hall of Fame. "Old Aches and Pains" played 20 seasons in the majors and managed one season in the majors. (Photo courtesy of Indianapolis Indians.)

VERN RAPP, MANAGER, 1969-75. Rapp guided the Indians for seven seasons and won 513 games, the second most in club history. He took the team to the playoffs twice and was named American Association Manager of the Year both seasons. He finished his Tribe career with a 513-452 mark. (Photo courtesy of Indianapolis Indians.)

ROCKY COLAVITO, OUTFIELDER, 1954-55. Colavito led the Tribe in home runs and RBI for two seasons before going onto a 14-year major league career. His 38 homers in 1954 is the highest single-season total in Indians history. His 68 homers are the second most in Indians history. (Photo courtesy of Indianapolis Indians.)

1961 INDIANS. The 1961 Indianapolis Indians won the American Association with an 86-64 record. The team included, from left to right: (seated) clubhouse boy Allen Smith and bat boy Clark Dickerson; (front row) business manager Max Schumacher, manager Ellis Deal, Joe Hicks, Len Johnston, Joe Gaines, Lamar Jacobs, Hilario Valdespino, player-coach Ted Beard, pitcher-coach Cloyd Boyer, and treasurer Robert Weimer; (middle row) Claude Osteen, Bob

38

Krop, Bob Miller, Ray Rippelmeyer, Greg Jancich, John Tsitouris, Don Rudolph, John Briggs, and promotion-publicity director Estel Freeman; (back row) Chet Boak, Bob Schmidt, Hiraldo Ruiz, Hal Bevan, Fred Hopke, Jim Snyder, Cliff Cook, Don Pavletich, and trainer Charley Saad. (Photo courtesy of Indianapolis Indians.)

GEORGE FOSTER, OUTFIELDER, 1973. Foster played one season with the Tribe before going onto an 18-year career in the majors that included three World Series. (Photo courtesy of Indianapolis Indians.)

KEN GRIFFEY, OUTFIELDER, 1973-74. Griffey led the team in hitting and the league in stolen bases in 1973. He was named as the Tribe's MVP and league's Rookie of the Year. Then he went to the majors for 17 seasons and played in two World Series. Fans recall seeing his son, Ken Jr., playing in the halls of Bush Stadium as a child. (Photo courtesy of Indianapolis Indians.)

NICK ESASKY, INFIELDER, 1981-83. Esasky was part of the American Association championship team in 1982. He went on to an eight-year career in the majors. (Photo courtesy of Jackie Dowling.)

SKEETER BARNES, PITCHER, 1981-83, 1985-86. Barnes pitched on two championship Indians teams. He then played for the Montreal Expos for three seasons. (Photo courtesy of Jackie Dowling.)

1974 Indians. The 1974 Indianapolis Indians won the American Association with a 78-57 record. The team, from left to right: (front row) president Max Schumacher, Ken Griffey, Tom Spencer, Joel Youngblood, manager Vern Rapp, Roger Freed, Ed Armbrister, and business manager Terry Stewart; (middle row) Will McEnaney, Dan Osborn, Rawly Eastwick, Pat

Zachary, Santo Alcala, Pat Darcy, Tom Carroll, Joaquin Andujar, and Dick Baney; (back row) groundskeeper Ike Ives, Jim Driscoll, Gene Dusan, Ray Knight, Arturo DeFreites, Junior Kennedy, Doug Flynn, Sonny Ruberto, and trainer Ron McClain. Bat boy Mark Storen is sitting up front. (Photo courtesy of Indianapolis Indians.)

RAZOR SHINES, INFIELDER, 1984-89, '91-93. Shines was a member of four straight championship teams and ranks among Indians career leaders in five categories: home runs (tie 2nd), RBI (2nd), runs (4th), games (4th), and doubles (5th). He was named team MVP in 1984. (Photo courtesy of Indianapolis Indians.)

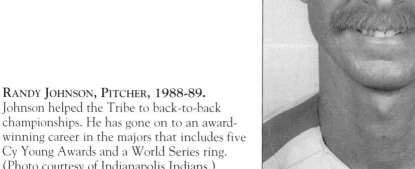

RANDY JOHNSON, PITCHER, 1988-89. Johnson helped the Tribe to back-to-back championships. He has gone on to an award-winning career in the majors that includes five Cy Young Awards and a World Series ring. (Photo courtesy of Indianapolis Indians.)

LARRY WALKER, OUTFIELDER, 1989. Walker helped the Indians to an American Association championship. Then he went onto a successful major league career that continues today. He was named National League MVP in 1997 and won the batting championship in 1998 with a .363 average. (Photo courtesy of Indianapolis Indians.)

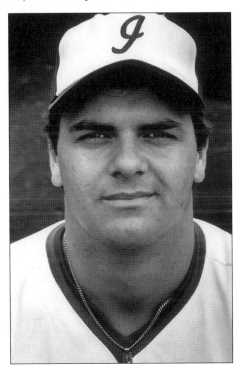

1988 INDIANS. The 1988 Indianapolis Indians won the American Association with an 89-53 record. Then the team won the playoffs. The team included, from left to right: (first row) Mel Houston, Tim Hulett, Johnny Paredes, Rex Hudler, Jack Daugherty, Razor Shines, Mike Smith, clubhouse manager Billy Neely, and stadium director Mike Tarrolly; (second row) president Max Schumacher, manager Joe Sparks, coach Mike Colbern, player-coach Nelson Norman, Nelson Santovenia, Wilfredo Tejada, Garrett Nago, pitching coach Joe Kerrigan, and assistant

general manager Cal Burleson; (third row) Steve Shirley, Sergio Valdez, Bob Sebra, Jeff Fischer, Brian Holman, Randy Johnson, Gary Wayne, Kurt Kepshire, Joe Hesketh, and Tim Barrett; (fourth row) groundskeeper Eddie Dick, ticket manager Mike Schneider, business manager Dan Stevens, Otis Nixon, Billy Moore, Ron Sheperd, Alonzo Powell, Mike Berger, trainer Tim McCormack, and director of special projects Bruce Schumacher. (Photo courtesy of Indianapolis Indians.)

ANDRES GALARRAGA, FIRST BASEMAN, 1985. Galarraga was named Rookie of the Year and to the American Association All-Star team after leading the team in runs (75), triples (8), homers (25), and RBI (87). His major league career continues today. (Photo courtesy of Indianapolis Indians.)

JOE SPARKS, MANAGER, 1986-88. Sparks guided the team to three straight American Association championships and was named league manager of the year three straight times. His 1988 club had the third-best single-season winning percentage (.627). (Photo courtesy of Indianapolis Indians.)

MOISES ALOU, OUTFIELDER, 1991. Alou played a season with the Indians before making his way back to the majors with Montreal. He has played eleven seasons in the majors for five different teams. (Photo courtesy of Jackie Dowling.)

1994 INDIANS. The 1994 Indianapolis Indians won the American Association with an 87-57 record. The team included, from left to right: (first row) Casey Candaele, Doug Jennings, Kurt Stillwell, Gary cooper, Keith Kessinger, Keith Gordon, Jamie Dismuke, and Rick Sellers; (second row) president Max Schumacher, manager Marc Bombard, Barry Lyons, Steve Pegues, Tim Costo, Jim Olander, pitching coach Mike Griffin, coach Jim Thrift, and assistant general manager Cal Burleson; (third row) Joe Roper, Brian Warren, Rich Sauveur, Jeffy Spradlin,

Terry Bross, Scott Service, Mike Ferry, Matt Grott, Rusty Kilgo, and Rich DeLucia; (back row) promotions coordinator Daryle Keith, stadium director Dan Madden, assistant stadium director Chuck Vonins, ticket manager Mike Schneider, clubhouse manager Bobby Smith, clubhouse manager Bobby Smith, business manager Doehrman, director of special projects Bruce Schumacher, trainer John Young, and bullpen coach Scott Young. (Photo courtesy of Indianapolis Indians.)

BRIAN DORSETT, CATCHER, 1993. Dorsett played for five seasons in the majors for four different teams before coming to the Indians. He had a great game at the beginning of the 1993 season in which he hit three home runs and six RBI in one game. "I never had that much power before," he recalled. He played on the 1993 championship team until the Cincinnati Reds called him up on July 1.

YMCA. Rowdie, the Indians mascot, leads the fans in the YMCA between innings. He is sometimes joined by "Macho Mike" Sullivan, an usher. The routine began at Bush Stadium and was carried over to Victory Field.

VICTORY FIELD. Victory Field is located in downtown Indianapolis, allowing for easy access to Indianapolis residents and visitors to the Circle City. The field is near the NCAA Hall of Champions, Indiana State Museum, White River Gardens, and the Indianapolis Zoo. Also, nearby is the sprawling campus of Indiana University/Purdue University Indianapolis. The field

got its name from the Indians' former home, which was named Victory Field from 1942 to 1967. "It's a beautiful ballpark, and it's part of one of the best sports downtowns anywhere in America," said Bob Costas. Downtown also features the RCA Dome and Conseco Fieldhouse.

TRYOUTS. Dave Jennings from the Cincinnati Reds talks to Mike Anderson of Chesterton during a tryout at Victory Field. The local news crew was on hand to tape the action. The Reds used to hold a yearly tryout at the ballpark when it had a contract with Indianapolis.

THE BEST MINOR LEAGUE STADIUM. Victory Field was built at a cost of $20 million and became the best minor league park in the nation according to *Baseball America* and *Sports Illustrated*. It opened on July 11, 1996, to a sellout crowd of 14,667. In 2001, the ballpark hosted the Triple-A All-Star Game. The stadium has 12,500 permanent stadium seats, a 1,000-seat bleacher and room for about 2,000 on the lawns in the outfield. The field also features 28 luxury suites, two party terraces, two suite lounges, and a party deck. The field has two picnic areas, lawn seating, televisions, and the "Hot Corner" Gift Shop. Public tours of the field are available during the season.

ENTERTAINMENT AT VICTORY FIELD. The scoreboard is a welcomed site to fans, who were used to viewing a manual scoreboard at the old Bush Stadium. The big screen informs fans of players coming to bat and serves as entertainment between innings with hat races, horse races and the like. The Indians also recognize birthdays, anniversaries and group outings. A ground level scoreboard in left field keeps fans apprised of other major and minor league games. Fans can also enjoy an interactive Speed Pitch, Pop-A-Shot, and face-painting stations. Tribe fries are especially liked by fans as well as pizza, hot dogs, burgers, chicken, and other baseball favorites. Andrew Lorraine warms up in the shadows.

MISS INDIANS. Jackie Dowling is joined at a game by Rob Purvis, a first-round draft pick by the Chicago White Sox. Dowling has been going to Indians games since the 1950s and is known by fans as Miss Indians. She keeps in touch with many former players.

PETE ROSE JR., INFIELDER, 1997-98. The son of Pete Rose played with the Indians before being called up by the Cincinnati Reds for a month in what some called a publicity stunt. He was originally drafted by the Baltimore Orioles. (Photo courtesy of Jackie Dowling.)

2000 INDIANS. The 2000 Indianapolis Indians won the International League and the Triple-A Championship. Team members included, from left to right: (front row) manager Steve Smith, Mickey Lopez, Lou Collier, Raul Casanova, Horacio Estrada, Ricardo Jordan, Damon Hollins, Norberto Martin, hitting coach Luis Salazar, and pitching coach Dwight Bernard; (middle row) clubhouse manager Jeff Rinaldi, trainer Paul Anderson, Rafaey Roque, Mike

Busby, Eric Ludwick, Jeff D'Amico, Bob Scanlan, Matt Luke, Greg Mix, Kurt Bierek, and strength and conditioning coach Sean Cochran; (back row) Brad Tyler, Jose Fernandez, Creighton Gubanich, Joe Crawford, Hector Ramirez, Allen Levrault, Everett Stuff, Rodney Bolton, Santiago Perez, and Scott Krause. (Photo courtesy of Indianapolis Indians.)

PAUL KONERKO, INFIELDER, 1998. Konerko played for a short time with the Indians in 1998 before being called up to the Reds. Cincinnati then traded him to the Chicago White Sox, where he has taken over at first base. He was originally drafted by the Los Angeles Dodgers.

MARK THOMPSON, PITCHER, 1999. Thompson came to the Indians for a short time in 1999 before the Reds traded him to St. Louis. He played seven years in the major leagues.

MIKE WALKER, PITCHER, 1997-98. Walker came to Indianapolis after five seasons in the majors with three different teams. He was originally drafted by the Cleveland Indians. (Photo courtesy of Jackie Dowling.)

VIPs. The Indians get their share of special visitors. Don Larson stopped by Victory Field in 1999 to visit with the staff and see the field. Larson, who was born in Indiana, is the only pitcher to throw a perfect game in the World Series. He never played with the Indians. (Photo courtesy of Jackie Dowling.)

AARON BOONE, THIRD BASE, 1997-99. Boone played for a couple seasons in Indianapolis before being promoted to the Cincinnati Reds, where he played in 2002. He is a third generation major league player. His brother, Brett, also plays in the majors.

JASON BERE, PITCHER, 1998. Bere played in Indianapolis while he was rehabbing from surgery. He was drafted in the 36th round by the Chicago White Sox in 1990, and has pitched in the majors for ten years. In 2002, he threw for the Chicago Cubs.

BRETT TOMKO, PITCHER, 1997 AND 1999. Tomko was drafted by the Reds and was promoted to the club in 1997. He pitched for a short time in Indianapolis in 1999. Then he was traded to Seattle. In 2002, he pitched for San Diego.

MAX SCHUMACHER, PRESIDENT AND CHAIRMAN OF THE BOARD. Schumacher has been with the club since 1957 when he was first hired as the ticket manager. He worked his way up the corporate ladder and took over as president in 1969. He earned American Association Executive of the Year honors in 1996. Then he was named chairman of the board in 1997. Under his leadership, he has brought 12 championship teams to Indianapolis. Schumacher's goal has been to bring low-cost family entertainment to the residents of Indianapolis. Attendance has risen to over 600,000 since the move to Victory Field. (Photo courtesy of Indianapolis Indians.)

BABE RUTH EXHIBIT. A fan checks out the Babe Ruth exhibit that came to Victory Field at the end of the 2002 season. The exhibit from the Babe Ruth Museum in Baltimore was at the stadium for three days, at the end of an 18-stadium tour. The exhibit featured the "called shot" home run at Wrigley Field in the 1932 World Series between the Yankees and the Cubs, with rare video footage of the actual at-bat.

THREE

The Federal League

IN 1913, the Federal League was formed as an independent league and the Indianapolis Hoosierfeds franchise was created. The league also placed teams in Chicago, Cleveland, Covington, Pittsburgh, and St. Louis. The Covington franchise later moved to Kansas City during the season. The minor league team played at Riverside Park. Some fans referred to the team as the "Hoofeds." Manager "Silent" Bill Phillips directed his club to first place in the new league with a 75-45 record, ten games better than its nearest competitor, the Cleveland Green Sox. Hoosierfeds' Bid Dolan led the league with a .346 batting average.

The Federal League decided to challenge Major League Baseball in 1914 by doing away with salary limits. That move allowed Indianapolis President J. Edward Krause to lure Edd Rousch, a future Hall of Famer, and pitcher Cy Faulkenberg, a former major leaguer, among others, from the majors and minors. Other franchises in the league included Baltimore, Brooklyn, Buffalo, Chicago, Kansas City, Pittsburgh, and St. Louis.

Faulkenberg won the opening game of the season on April 23, 1914, over Mordecai "Three Finger" Brown's St. Louis Feds, 7-3. Perhaps it was an omen of what was to come as Faulkenberg helped lead the team to a championship with his 25 victories. The team ended the season with an 88-65 record, just ahead of the Chicago Whales, which was led by player-manager Joe Tinker. Bill Phillips managed the club. Benny Kauff led the league in three categories: batting average (.370), runs (120), and hits (211). Frank LaPorte knocked in the 107 runs. Bill McKechnie would make a name for himself in the majors.

The success of the team was dashed the next season as the team was sold and moved to Newark, New Jersey. The Federal League lasted just one more year, and major league ball is yet to return to the Circle City. Indianapolis has continued with a successful minor league franchise—the Indianapolis Indians.

In 1984, Major League Baseball was talking expansion and Indianapolis was interested. The mayor appointed a committee, but it didn't have any money. So Art Angotti and a group of investors secured $80 million in financing to form the Indianapolis Arrows, Inc.

At first, the group thought the Hoosier Dome could be used for a team. The Dome had been built to lure the Baltimore Colts and not a baseball team. "Adaptability of the Hoosier Dome was a problem because it was not clear if it could accommodate baseball," explained Angotti. "Once it was realized that it could not, then we had a big hole in our presentation."

Then some of the people in the ownership group began to take unusual steps, Angotti added. And Channel 4, a local TV investor, filed for bankruptcy. The small size of the market was also a problem. The dreams of the entrepreneurs turned into a nightmare.

Indianapolis may never get a major league franchise, since baseball is now thinking about shrinking due to the poor economics of smaller markets, Angotti added.

Cy Falkenberg, Pitcher for Indianapolis Federals, 1914. Falkenberg was a former major league pitcher before jumping ship and joining the Federal League. He led the Indians to the championship in 1914 with his 25 victories. (Photo courtesy of the National Baseball Hall of Fame Library, Cooperstown, NY.)

EDD ROUSH, OUTFIELDER FOR INDIANAPOLIS FEDERALS, 1914. Roush came from the Chicago White Sox to the team. With Indianapolis, he played in 74 games and hit .325 on the season. He stayed in the league for another season before going on to an 18-year career in the majors. His .323 lifetime batting average helped him to a spot in the Hall of Fame in 1962.

CARR, INDIANAPOLIS

CHARLIE CARR, FIRST BASEMAN FOR INDIANAPOLIS FEDERALS, 1914. Carr played six years in the National League. His last was in 1906 when he hit just .191 for Cincinnati. He did a lot better for Indianapolis as he hit .293 and clotted three homers.

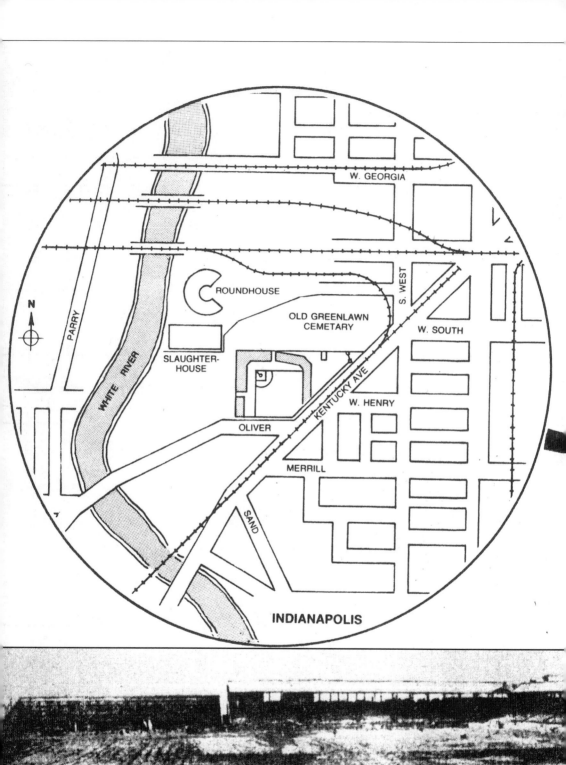

HOOSIER PARK. The Indianapolis Federal built Hoosier Park just south of Old Greenlawn Cemetery near Kentucky Ave. The park could seat 20,000. Made of concrete, steel and wood,

)ATA

nsions (estimated): LF 375', CF 400', RF 310'

ing capacity: 20,000

bination concrete, steel & wood

of construction: $100,000 - $250,000

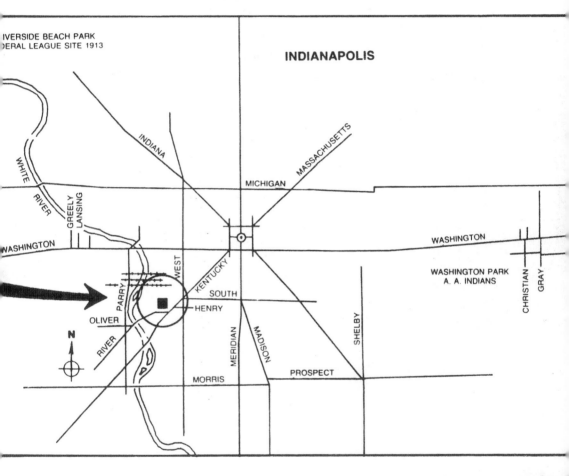

the outfield dimensions were 375 feet in left, 400 feet in center, and 310 feet in right.

Cracker Jack
BALL PLAYERS

KAISERLING, INDIANAPOLIS-FEDERALS

GEORGE KAISERLING, PITCHER FOR INDIANAPOLIS FEDERALS, 1914. Kaiserling got his start in professional ball with Indianapolis. The right-hander posted a 17-10 record that year. The next season he went to Newark with the team and was less successful with a 13-14 record. When the league ended, so did his major league career.

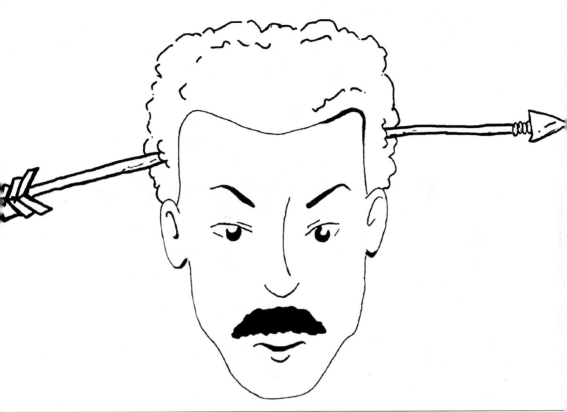

INDIANAPOLIS ARROWS. The attempt to bring the Arrows to Indianapolis failed. (Art courtesy of Randi Madden.)

HOLY COW! Harry Caray (left), the voice of the Chicago Cubs, tried to help Art Angotti (right) bring a major league franchise to Indianapolis. Caray came to Indianapolis to encourage the city to purchase an existing baseball team. The new team would be named the Arrows, which kept with the Indians theme the city had going for it for such a long time.

FOUR

Black Baseball

SOON AFTER the Civil War, African-Americans turned to baseball as recreation in Indianapolis. The first evidence of organized Negro teams came as early as the summer of 1867. As the population grew in the capital city, so did the interest in Black baseball. By the turn of the century, that interest reached the professional level and the Colored Baseball League was formed in July 1902. However, the league folded two months later. Teams such as the Indianapolis Unions and the Indianapolis ABCs, from that short-lived league, continued to play. The ABCs were so named from their affiliation with the American Brewing Company. In 1905, the ABCs played a double-header exhibition at Northwestern Baseball Park during the Great Emancipation Celebration. The following year, the ABCs played against the Nebraska Full Blooded Indians and won 9-8. The Black team also played other local semi-professional teams named the Indianapolis Crescents and Indianapolis Reserves.

The ABCs experienced sagging attendance in 1911 and held several promotions to attract fans. One included a female pitcher. She tossed a few innings for Louisville in a game against the ABCs. A boxing match preceded another contest. The following year, the owner of the team, Randolph Butler, sold the team to Thomas A. Bowser, a white Indianapolis bail bondsman. The team manager, George Abrams, quit the team in protest and formed his own team, the X-ABCs, whose name he later changed to Abrams Giants. He came to his senses the next year and returned to the ABCs. Another ownership change came in 1914 when Charles Isam Taylor bought half interest in the team. C.I., as he liked to be called, brought with him some talented players, including Dizzy Dismukes, George Brown, Morten "Morty" Clark, George Shively, and Bingo DeMoss. Taylor's brothers, James and Ben, also played for the team. He also signed a great local player, Oscar Charleston, a future Hall of Famer. All that talent led the ABCs to a disputed "Colored Championship Series" over the Chicago American Giants in 1916.

The First World War shortened the next three seasons for the ABCs. During those years, the team played some military opponents—the local Speedway Aviators and Camp Grant from Rockford, Illinois. Some team members were also called to the war themselves.

After the war, the ABCs joined the Negro National League when it was formed in 1920. Taylor was named as the league's vice president. Their first game was on May 2 and some six thousand fans watched the ABCs beat the Chicago Giants. The team played well and finished second that season. The Indianapolis franchise dropped to fifth the next season. Then Taylor passed away and left the team to his wife. The team rebounded to its best ever season record in 1922 (46-33) to finish second again. In 1923, the ABCs caught fire at the beginning season and charged into first with an 11-1 record. That fire burned out, however, and the Kansas City Monarchs won the league championship. Charleston, Frank Warfield, and Elvis Holland became known as the "Indianapolis Bunch." A mass exodus occurred in 1924 and the team fell out of the league. The ABCs returned for three more seasons before dropping out again due to lack of funds. It returned to the league again once more in 1931.

The Depression spelled the end of the Negro National League after 1931, but other Negro leagues continued, so the ABCs joined the Negro Southern League and finished with a 14-19 record in 1932. The following year, the Chicago American Giants moved to Indianapolis after they had problems finding a field to play on in the "Windy City." The team continued to wear Chicago uniforms and played for a season before moving back to "Shy Town." That cavity was soon filled with a team called the Monarchs. Other semi-pro teams sprung up in the mid-1930s, including the Zulu Cannibal Giants, a team who wore shirts and head dresses like the African tribe. Beer became legal again in 1934 and some brewery teams started playing semi-pro ball. The Sterling Beers were lead by former Chicago White Sox pitcher Reb Russell and managed by Clyde Hoffa. Later came the Gold Medal Brewery team. By 1939, several factories had teams, such as the Kingan Packers. The last time the ABCs suited up came in 1940 as a semi-pro team.

The Indianapolis Athletics were born in 1937 as part of the Negro American League. The team played so poorly on the field that they didn't last a season in the NAL. A revived ABCs team joined the league in 1938, but moved to St. Louis the next season. They were quickly replaced by the Atlanta Black Crackers, who moved into Indianapolis and played as the ABCs for a short time in 1939. Then the Indianapolis Crawfords joined the league in 1940 when Charleston decided to move his Toledo team to his hometown. That move was brief.

Another war came in 1941. Perry Stadium was renamed Victory Field. The field was once used during the war for the fifth game of the Negro World Series between the Homestead Grays and the Birmingham Black Barons.

The Ethiopian Clowns adopted Indianapolis as their home city in 1944 when the team joined the Negro American League. The team dropped its on-field antics—such as "shadow ball"—and became serious about playing. They adopted the name of Indianapolis-Cincinnati Clowns. The team also looked for talented players, like Willie "the Devil" Wells, who played in 1947. Wells would later find a spot in the Baseball Hall of Fame.

The talented Clowns won the NAL pennant in 1950 and 1951. Then they won the league championship series over the Birmingham Black Barons in 1952. Hank Aaron played for the Clowns for two months early in the season before signing a contract with the Boston Braves. Ironically, he never actually played a game in the Circle City as most Clowns' games were on the road.

In 1953, the team signed the first woman to play in professional black baseball—Toni Stone. Although signed as a gate attraction, she played second base and hit a respectable .243. The following year the Clowns signed two other women: Mamie "Peanut" Johnson and Connie Morgan. Morgan replaced Stone at second base. Johnson was used as a pitcher and utility player. "I threw anything I needed to throw," Johnson commented on a trip back to Indianapolis in 2002.

"She even tried a knuckleball," added her catcher, Art Hamilton.

Oscar Charleston joined the Clowns in 1954 and managed it to the NAL title with a 43-22 mark. After the season, Charleston suffered a stroke and died in Philadelphia. The Indianapolis Clowns became the Harlem Globetrotters of baseball and went back to clowning around. The Clowns played only about four games a year in Indianapolis at Bush Stadium. The team became integrated and played until 1989. The Clowns were the last great barnstorming team and marked the end of an era.

Charleston was honored in 1998 when Indianapolis dedicated a park in his name.

ROAD TRIP. The Indianapolis ABCs traveled by car to get to games in other cities. Their dog enjoyed the ride as well. (Photo courtesy of Larry Lester.)

INDIANAPOLIS ABCS. The 1915 Indianapolis ABCs included, from left to right: (front row) outfielder George Shivey and pitcher James Jeffries; (middle row) outfielder Oscar Charleston, pitcher Louis "Dicta" Johnson, manager C.I. Taylor, outfielder Jimmie Lyons, and third

baseman Todd Allen; (back row) catcher Russell Powell, first baseman Ben Taylor, pitcher Dick "Cannonball" Redding, second baseman Elwood "Bingo" DeMoss, shortstop Morten "Morty" Clark, and catcher Dan Kennard. (Photo courtesy of Jay Sanford.)

SMALL CLOWN. Dero Austin was so short—two-foot-seven—that he didn't have to get on his knees to catch the ball. The Indianapolis Clowns had quite a few characters like Dero. The players would also perform a baseball pantomime called "Shadow Ball," in which they took infield practice with an imaginary baseball. The crowd loved it. (Photo courtesy of Larry Lester.)

BARNSTORMING. The Indianapolis Clowns traveled by bus all over the country to play games. Although the team carried the name Indianapolis, they only played in the Circle City about four times a year. The rest of the time they were on the road. The Clowns were the last barnstorming team in the country. (Photo courtesy of Larry Lester.)

OSCAR CHARLESTON. Charleston played seven seasons for the Indianapolis ABCs and managed the team in 1954. He also managed the Indianapolis Crawfords in 1940. He began with the ABCs a batboy when he was a child. After a stint with the Army, he returned as a player. He became one of the best African-American players ever and later a manager. In 1976, he was named to the National Baseball Hall of Fame. (Photo courtesy of Larry Lester.)

REUNION. Mamie "Peanut" Johnson, a pitcher with the Indianapolis Clowns, returned to Indianapolis in 2002 for the first time since her playing days. She was joined by her catcher, Art Hamilton. The two threw out the first pitch at an Indianapolis Indians game at Victory Field.

Left to right:
Bunny Downs (Traveling Secretary),
Ray Neil, Toni Stone, Albert "Buster" Haywood
Indianapolis Clowns, Circa 1946-1948

An Illustrated History of
NEGRO LEAGUES BASEBALL
Exhibition June 8 - July 16, 2002

NCAA
Hall of Champions
It's the Journey

EXHIBIT. The NCAA Hall of Champions held an exhibit of Negro League Baseball in 2002 from June 8 to July 16. The material was on loan from the Negro League Baseball Museum in Kansas City.

OLD PHOTOS. A visitor to the Negro League Baseball exhibit at the NCAA Hall of Champions looks over images on display. Also on display were uniforms and other memorabilia.

HANK AARON. Before entering the major leagues, Hank Aaron played a couple of months for the Indianapolis Clowns. His photo was on display at the NCAA Hall of Champions exhibit.

LOCKERS. Lockers and uniforms from the Negro Leagues were on display at the NCAA Hall of Fame Negro League Baseball Exhibit in 2002. The locker on the left contained items from Oscar Charleston, legendary player and manager of the Indianapolis ABCs. On the right is the locker of Hall-of-Fame shortstop John "Pop" Lloyd, star of the Negro Leagues who Babe Ruth reportedly commented was the greatest player of all time. Lloyd played and managed in the Negro Leagues from 1906 to 1932. He was considered the greatest shortstop of his time, black or white.

UNIFORM. An Indianapolis Clowns uniform was on display at the NCAA Hall of Fame exhibit.

FIVE
Semi-Pro Baseball

SEMI-PROFESSIONAL BASEBALL—good players who are paid a small amount or nothing at all for their services—began in Indianapolis 1867 and continues today. "Amateur baseball is making a comeback," said Commissioner Brian Drake of the Men's Senior Baseball League in Indianapolis.

Semi-pro, also known as factory or industrial baseball, began when hotels, barber shops, factories, and other business establishments formed teams from their workforce to compete with other such teams. Semi-pro teams filled the void when Indianapolis residents had no professional teams to root for. Ball teams used to gather in front of Igoe's cigar store at Meridian and Washington Streets to arrange games. Teams named the Shamrocks, Orientals and Grand Avenue competed in the days of seven balls and three strikes. Amos Rusie, a Hall-of-Fame player, got his very start with Grand Avenue, which played every weekend for three seasons. Pitchers threw from a flat, rectangular box only 45 feet from home plate. Even some women's teams played the sport back then. One was called the Star Bloomer Girls Base Ball Club and played at 627 West Michigan Street. As enough teams were formed, leagues were formed and the process became more formal.

Baseball was even played on roller skates. In September 1885, the Virginia Avenues played the Beacons on skates at the Virginia Avenue rink. Indoor baseball was also played in Indianapolis a few years later. The sport was developed by George Hancock in Chicago around 1890. The ball was much larger and softer than a regular baseball and the bats were smaller. Players wore rubber soled shoes instead of spikes. The sport spread to other parts of the state as well. Nowadays, we call the sport softball and play it outside.

As the 1900s rolled around, more and more businesses followed the practice. The Indianapolis Colts played semi-pro ball on Sundays in the West Washington Park and skirted Blue Laws prohibiting Sunday baseball by not charging admission. Instead, they charged for programs. Then in 1911, the Indianapolis Amateur Baseball Association was formed. One of the founding fathers was Carl C. Callahan. Teams from Riddlen Drug Store, Rupps Drug Store, and the Hotel Severin participated, among others. Walter J. Sauter played for Hotel Severin; George Sims played with Riddlen; and Willie McDonnell, Joe Meo and Henry Peters played for Rupps.

In 1926, the Indianapolis Power & Light Company baseball team won the industrial championship of the United States. The team was so good that it won every game it played in the Capitol City League. Teams played at Riverside Park. Then they traveled to Philadelphia and won the national crown before 10,000 fans at Sesquicentennial Stadium. The IPL team performed the feat again in 1928 in Detroit. "It was the high class of semi-pro ball," explained Norm Beplay, who joined the team in 1929 after playing for the Illinois Central Railroad team. The middle infielder played for the team until 1931, when the Depression spelled the end to the team and the league. He joined an Indianapolis Kotsky team and was paid $10 to $15 a game. Kotsky bought the players uniforms, jackets, equipment, and provided all the transportation. "Those were great days," recalled Beplay, now in his nineties.

When Prohibition ended, beer and whiskey teams popped up in Indianapolis and around the state. Beplay turned to managing the Gold Medal Beer team until 1945. In 1961, the association celebrated its 50th anniversary. Teams included WHS Electric, South Side Saints, Southeastern Supply, and Mallory A.A. The popularity of the league began to dwindle after that. By the late 1970s, little evidence of factory ball existed. The Eastside Indians and Smith Electric were two of the last semi-pro teams in existence.

The Men's Senior Baseball League (MSBL) began as a four-team league in Long Island, New York, in the 1980s. By 1990, the league had spread to Indianapolis thanks to local founder Steve Baertschi and a group of others, who said they were extras in the movie "Eight Men Out," when the inspiration came to play again. The first season featured nine teams in the 30-plus division. The popularity of the league grew rapidly in the Circle City and soon there were more teams and divisions. By 1997, the league featured three divisions and became known as one of the strongest programs in the nation. By 2002, a dozen teams competed in the 18-plus (known as the Men's Adult Baseball League) and 30-plus divisions, while a handful of teams played at the 40-plus level. That ranked Indianapolis as the 11th largest league of 350 leagues in the nation. The Indianapolis league featured some 450 players in 2002. Nationwide, the organization has grown to 44,000!

Most teams compete on high school or college baseball fields on Sundays, but the 40-plus league plays during the weekdays at a diamond at the Central Regional Little League headquarters in Lawrence. Occasionally, teams play at Victory Field and Cinergy Field. In 2000, the league hosted its first Labor Day Regional Tournament, featuring teams from all over the Midwest. The Detroit Dodgers defeated the Chicago Oaks for the title.

The players in the league come with all sorts of backgrounds. A few of the players have professional experience in the minors. The Braves in the 30-plus division sport three such players. Dave Overstreet, now 50, played nine years in the minors with the Cincinnati Reds. He was signed out of a tryout camp by the Reds in September 1970. The closest he got to making it to the majors was being on the Reds 40-man roster. He played a season with the Indianapolis Indians in 1974. Scott Leverenz, 49, was drafted by the Pirates in 1974 in the 19th round. He played two-and-half years in the minors. "I blew up my left knee," explained the first baseman. Overstreet and Leverenz played together at Lawrence Central High School before turning pro. Mike Lexa was drafted by the Minnesota Twins in the 23rd round in 1986 and played three years in the minors. Besides the former pros, the league is filled with former college players, including Lieutenant Governor Joe Kernan, who was a catcher with Notre Dame. He played in the 40-plus league in 2002 with the Astros.

Instead of getting paid to play, players have to pay to play. The fee to enter a team in the league is about $3,000, or $225 for an individual. Players may also need to pay for their uniform, as only a few companies still sponsor teams. One sponsor in 2002 was Methodist Sports Medicine.

The strongest team in the 30-plus Division has been the Giants, who won the MSBL World Series in 1999 and was runner-up in 2000. They've done so well in the national championship by recruiting the services of some former pros, like Mark Davis, a Cy Young Award winner in the majors. The team picked up the players on waivers from other MSBL teams before the championships. The Giants have won division championships six out of the last seven years. "We've had the same core group the last nine years," explained manager Joe Manship. "It keeps the chemistry going."

The league's motto: "Don't Go Soft—Play Hardball!"

90

EARLY SEMI-PRO TEAM. The Castleton area of Indianapolis fielded this team of ballplayers in 1917. Back then, the area was nothing but farmland. Today, the area is known for its shopping district and Castleton Square Mall. This photo of the team hangs on the wall of a Meijer store.

OUT AT FIRST! Joel Manship, the manager of the Giants, crosses the bag too late as Braves' Scott Leverenz, a former minor league player, takes the throw. Several ex-minor league players play in the Indianapolis league.

SMALL CROWDS. The Braves' Dave Overstreet takes a swipe at a pitch during a game against the Giants as umpire Kerry Britt decides on the call and Dean Hill makes the catch. Overstreet spent nine years in the minor leagues, including a trip to the Indianapolis Indians in 1974. The Mens Senior Baseball League doesn't attract many fans, just family, but the players don't care. They are there to experience the game again like they did when they were in their childhood.

LEFTY HURLER. John Simpson of the Giants delivers a pitch during a playoff game against the Braves. The left-handed pitcher fooled many batters with his super slow curveball. The Giants ended up beating the Braves, 5-2. The Giants have the winningest team in the Mens Senior Baseball League and won the championship again in 2002.

Lt. Governor. Lieutenant Governor Joe Kernan warms up before a game. The fifty-six year old played third base for the Astros in the 40-plus league. Kernan was a catcher at Notre Dame in his college days.

CAPTAIN. Harv Austin gives instructions to his 40-plus Pirates before they take the field in the playoffs. At age 59, Austin still plays with the best of them.

COMMISSIONER. Brian Drake was the commissioner for the Men's Adult Baseball League in 2002. He also played for a couple of teams in the different divisions of the league.

CONSECO CUBS. The Conseco Cubs sponsored a team in the Mens Adult Baseball League in the 18-plus division in 1999. Some of the players had experience in college baseball. Conseco

later dropped its sponsorship after the company ran into financial trouble. (Photo courtesy of Patrick Stewart.)

HE SCORES! Patrick Stewart of the Conseco Cubs scores a run during a game at Victory Field, home of the Indianapolis Indians. Stewart, whose grandfather played for the Chicago Colts in 1895, played several years in the Mens Adult Baseball League.

Six

Youth Baseball

Little League Baseball

Little League Baseball was founded in Williamsport, Pennsylvania, by Carl E. Stotz in 1939. The league spread slowly across the country and the first teams began showing up in Indianapolis by 1951. The Fairgrounds League was the first formed and soon there were leagues throughout the city.

State championships began being held in 1958. The only Indianapolis team to win the Indiana championship was the Warren Township Nationals in 1984. Nearby Southport made the trip in 1984 and Center Grove (Greenwood) in 1980.

The Road to Williamsport got a little shorter for Indiana teams in 1989 as the city landed the permanent home for Central Region playoffs. Up until that time, the playoffs roamed around the Midwest like gypsies. Several charitable groups made it possible: Developer Gene B. Glick donated the land, which now bears his name, and Eli Lilly Endowment gave a $250,000 grant. That was enough to convince Little League officials to use Indianapolis instead of Chicago.

The site has been turned into a field of dreams for a dozen teams from around the Midwest to compete each year. Brownsburg, a suburb of Indianapolis, has nearly made the site its own home as it won back-to-back-to-back-to-back Indiana championships from 1999 to 2002. The team won the Midwest Regional in 2001 and traveled to Williamsport, but was eliminated there. In 2002, the team fell one game short of going to Williamsport again as the Bulldogs lost to Kentucky, who ended up winning the Little League World Series. So Coach Rick Green started to tell people that his team was beat by the world champions, according to his son Randy.

The baseball complex ranks up there with major league spring training sites with a dormitory, several fields, offices, nurse's quarters, a cafeteria, press box, swimming pool, tennis courts, and basketball courts. The sweet smell of cotton candy permeates the stands that can accommodate up to 2,000 fans.

The Opening Ceremonies in 2002 featured a precise performance by the Marion County Motorcycle team and the arrival of Dugout, the Little League mascot, from Williamsport, courtesy of a helicopter ride from the Indiana State Police.

Continental Amateur Baseball Association

In competition with Little League baseball in central Indiana is the Continental Amateur

Baseball Association (CABA). Boys ages 7 to 12 compete against each other as independent teams in May and June then come together for a World Series in Noblesville in late July.

Rules are a little different than Little League and are closer to what is used in the majors. The mound and bases are farther back than Little League, too. "It makes it more like real baseball," explained Jim Reboulet, coach of the Hamilton Southeast Royals. Boys from Fishers, a suburb of Indianapolis, play on the team. Some 30 to 40 teams compete in the Indianapolis area.

Reboulet is the brother of pitcher Jeff Reboulet, a pitcher for the Los Angeles Dodgers. His philosophy is not always on winning. "I don't put a lot of emphasis on wins and losses," he commented. "I try to give players opportunities." He only places some emphasis on winning when tournament time rolls around. His team finished sixth in the World Series.

AMERICAN LEGION BASEBALL

American Legion Baseball (ALB) programs began at Indianapolis posts back in 1928. The first chairman was Bob Bushee of Osslan, and he was faced with a problematic baseball player by the name of Gisolo in Blanford. The problem was Gisolo's first name—Margaret. The Legion tried to dismiss the girl, but left it up to Judge Kenesaw Mountain Landis, the major league baseball commissioner. He couldn't find anything in the new rules that disallowed her from playing, so he ruled in her favor. Ironically, Gisolo and her teammates went on to beat Fort Benjamin Harrison Post No. 40, an Indianapolis post, and then whipped Gary in the final game to win the state championship. The following year an embarrassed National Americanism Commission prohibited girls from playing junior baseball. Today, only one Indianapolis post has an American Legion team, as many players have opted to play in the Indianapolis Amateur Baseball Association.

In the 1990s, Indianapolis teams began dropping out of ALB programs due to a number of problems. "They couldn't get kids because high schools forbid their players to play on other programs," explained Denise Domogalik, American Legion of Indiana.

The coach of the only remaining team in Indianapolis—Wayne Post 64-disagreed. "I think the traveling all-stars teams are to blame," commented Phil Webster. Webster named the Indiana Bulls, Stars and Mavericks as the culprits, because they take boys all over the state and country for games. He also blames the Legion for too much bureaucracy. He said their rules were cumbersome and there was too much paperwork. Webster also blamed a limited budget by some Legion posts, while others seem to have unlimited funds. However, he says he gets enough and that's why he will continue the team, which is made up of boys from Decatur Central High School, where he is the baseball coach. In the ten years that Webster has coached Legion ball, he's won the sectionals three times. His best team posted a 21-8 record, but the 2002 team was 11-14.

INDIANA HIGH SCHOOLS

The Indiana High School Athletic Association (IHSAA) held its first state finals in baseball in 1912. South Bend won the championship and Indianapolis Manual finished second. It wasn't until 1917 that the next championship was held. Indianapolis Arsenal Tech destroyed Kewanna 12-2 for the title. The finals went into a long hibernation and began again on a regular basis in 1967. The state finals have been held in Indianapolis in all but three years. The finals were held at Bush Stadium (home of the Indianapolis Indians) on 16th Street until 1996, when the series was moved to Victory Field downtown. In 1998, the IHSAA moved to a four-class system. Nearly four hundred schools participate in the single-elimination tournament each year.

In the history of the event, Indianapolis high schools can claim only three championships: Ben Davis in 1981, Park Tudor in 1999, and Indianapolis Cathedral in 2001. More Indy teams have finished in second: Arlington in 1967, Marshall in 1974 and 1975, Roncalli in 1982, and

Lawrence North in 1999.

The IHSAA also presents the L.V. Philips Mental Attitude Award each year to the player who excels in mental attitude, leadership, and athletic ability. Award winners from Indianapolis have been David Highmark from North Central in 1970, Gene "Bucky" Autry from Ben Davis in 1981, Tal Short from Lawrence North in 1999, and Bill Potter from Indianapolis Cathedral in 2001.

JUNIOR BASEBALL

Not long after the Second World War began, Junior Baseball got its start in Indianapolis. The goal of the organization was to give boys the opportunity to play organized baseball in areas where neighborhoods can't afford to pay national franchise fees. In other words, it was a poor man's Little League.

The Indianapolis Parks Department sponsored the program, which spread throughout Marion county and the state, so it became successful in combating delinquency during the summer months. The program's motto: "A Busy Boy is Never a Problem." Back in the early days of the program, teams would end the season with an all-star series in old Victory Field.

The program dropped off in the 1970s in the inner city as funding dried up. Former minor leaguer Milton Thompson set out to right the ship and bring baseball back to the inner city. He went to Lilly Endowment, the Indianapolis Indians and other organizations to help fund a new program. "We grew from there," he explained. He also went to high school and college coaches for their assistance. He landed a stadium deal with Marion College and a partnership with the Indianapolis Parks Department. What he finally wound up with was the Indianapolis Amateur Baseball Association. Major League Baseball also came around with a program called Reviving Baseball in Inner Cities (RBI) in the early 1990s to help disadvantaged players in Indianapolis.

In 2002, the various programs in the city involving some seven thousand youths were clumped together under a new name: Play Ball Indiana. The new name covers three baseball programs in the city: IABA High School Leagues, Mid-America Baseball Association, and RBI Indianapolis. "The hope is that Play Ball Indiana will be a better umbrella name for our various programs," explained executive director Michael Lennox, "and will ultimately help us do a better job raising the money needed to create baseball and softball opportunities for the young people in our community."

Probably the most successful traveling team program belongs to the Indiana Bulls. Founded in 1991, the team has been the launching pad for a number of players who have made it to the majors. Scott Rolen played for the Bulls in 1993 and he wound up as the National League Rookie of the Year in 1997. His teammate was Todd Dunwoody, who blazed his own path to the majors. More than twenty alumni have played in the majors.

INDIANAPOLIS-SCARBOROUGH PEACE GAMES

Baseball has been part of the Indianapolis-Scarborough Peace Games each year since the games began in 1973. The official proclamation of the event's name occurred on the very day that the Vietnam Peace Treaty was signed by President Richard Nixon—hence "Peace Games." The idea for the games came from the Canusa Games, which originated in Flint, Michigan, and Hamilton, Ontario, in 1957. In 2002, Indianapolis hosted the 30th annual Peace Games and won the baseball competition, four games to two. Baseball was played at three different sites in 2002 in the Circle City as three age groups competed: 9-12, 13-14 and 15-16. The games in alternate years are held in Scarborough, Canada, a suburb of Toronto.

Over the past 30 years, Indy Parks & Recreation has involved about 30,000 children and adults in the Peace Games. The international multi-sport event featured 13 events in 2002, playing with the theme "Building International Friendship through Competition." The competition is funded through donations and supported by volunteers.

OPENING CEREMONIES. The Brownsburg Bulldogs carry the Indiana State Champions flag to open the Central Region Little League playoffs in Lawrence. The team ended up finishing second in the playoffs in 2002.

BIG SWING. Randy Green of the Brownsburg Bulldogs takes a big swing at the ball during the Central Region Little League playoffs. He started playing baseball when he was four years old. "I've just loved the game," he said.

FAN SUPPORT. Many fans came out to watch Brownsburg play in the Central Region playoffs in 2002. Many wore T-Shirts that told about the team's success with back-to-back-to-back-to-back Indiana championships from 1999 to 2002.

SAFELY HOME. A Jasper High School player slides safely into home during the 1999 Indiana High School Athletic Association state finals at Victory Field.

ON DECK. Chad Liter readies to go up to bat at the Indiana High School finals. Liter was drafted by the Colorado Rockies in 1999.

FIRE AWAY! A pitcher on the Hamilton SE Royals lets go of a pitch. The team of 11 year olds competes in the Continental Amateur Baseball Association. (Photo courtesy of Rory Underwood.)

SAFE AT THIRD. A Hamilton SE Royals player slides safely at first as the third baseman from the Munson Mudhens awaits the throw. (Photo courtesy of Rory Underwood.)

SEVEN

Collegiate Baseball

PAN AM GAMES

Indianapolis lived up to its title as the amateur sports capital of the United States when it decided to host the Tenth Pan American Games in 1987. Getting the games was an accomplishment for the city, and getting Cuba to compete was an even greater reward. The competition was held over seventeen days in August with baseball games being held for the twelve nations at Bush Stadium, the home of the Indianapolis Indians, who went on a long road trip during that spell. The old stadium, which was built in 1931, was given a $148,000 facelift for the games.

The Cuban team stirred up emotions when it played and demonstrators from Cuba Independiente y Democratica caused a stir at Bush Stadium. The United States team, featuring the best college athletes in the nation, also caused a stir as it defeated Cuba 6-4 with a dramatic ninth-inning homer by Ty Griffin. However, Cuba had the last laugh as they beat the U.S. squad 13-9 in the final game to take the Gold Medal.

Pitcher Jim Abbott from Michigan University led the team to a silver medal. He started ten games and finished with an earned run average of 1.70. Attendance for the series was 61,666 for twenty-two sessions held at the stadium.

BUTLER UNIVERSITY

Butler University got its start in baseball in 1877, but not by playing the game. Instead, a professor there became involved in a controversy with the Indianapolis Blues, the local professional team.

When Blues pitcher Eddie "The Only" Nolan claimed he had a great curveball, Professor David Starr Jordan questioned the pitch and thought it was contrary to nature. He thought an optical illusion was involved. Butler's faculty even supported Dr. Jordan's position. So the Indianapolis team challenged Dr. Jordan to a demonstration. The test was made at a fire station. Two poles were placed a few feet apart and across them was stretched a piece of paper. About ten feet back were placed two other poles also plastered with paper. Nolan pitched a ball powdered with chalk through the two sheets of paper so the professor could trace the route. Sure enough, it was a curve. Dr. Jordan wouldn't have believed it if he hadn't seen it with his own eyes.

The university began a baseball program in 1901 when Dr. Walter Kelly coached the team to a 1-2 record. The team played less than ten games a season until Paul "Tony" Hinkle took over the team in 1921. He turned the program around. The Bulldogs became winners a majority of the time after that. Hinkle would guide the program for 38 more seasons, and his 1969 team was co-champs of the Indiana Collegiate Conference, the year before he retired. The team was co-champs again in 1974 under Tom Warner. Then Scott Neal took the team to the top of the Heartland Collegiate Conference in 1979 and 1980. After ten losing seasons, Neal was replaced by current coach Steve Farley. Farley turned the struggling program into a winner again and his team has won four Midwestern Collegiate Conferences during his eleven seasons. The Bulldogs have four winning seasons in the past five years and have recorded more than thirty wins in two of the past four years, including a school record thirty-three wins in 1998.

Farley has had thirty-eight players earn all-conference honors and thirteen players sign professional contracts. Butler pitcher Pat Neshek was selected in the sixth round of the Major League Baseball First-Year Player Draft by the Minnesota Twins in 2002. It made him the highest selected player in Butler history. And Butler senior John Corcoran, who was named Co-Pitcher of the Year in the Horizon League in 2002, signed a free agent contract with the Seattle Mariners.

Indiana University/Purdue University at Indianapolis

Baseball lasted 21 years as a varsity sport at Indiana University/Purdue University at Indianapolis. Baseball replaced golf as a varsity sport during the 1979-80 campaign. The program lasted until the 2001 season and was discontinued due to financial reasons. The team had to rent a facility off campus to play home games, and also had to spend a considerable amount for travel with a large roster of players. The poor record the team amassed had nothing to do with the demise of the sport, according to the college. The team had only seven winning seasons during its 21 years of existence. Its worst performance came in 1995 when the team went 3-55. However, it did have some winning seasons.

University of Indianapolis

The University of Indianapolis finished 2002 with a 31-21 record and second in the Great Lakes Valley Conference. After the season, senior pitcher Rick Hummel was drafted in the 32nd round of the Major League Baseball 2002 First-Year Player Draft by the Chicago White Sox. He agreed to terms and reported to the White Sox complex in Tucson, Arizona.

The Greyhounds are coached by Gary Vaught, who started coaching there in 1995. He took the team to the Division II College World Series for the first time in 2000 and the team finished third.

Opposite, Top: **Logo.** The Pan Am Games uses this logo, which was used on everything, including the pin this was taken from.

Opposite, Bottom: **Baseball Pin.** The Pan Am Games issued this pin for baseball.

The Tenth
Pan American Games
Indianapolis
7–23 August 1987

The Official
Pictograms of the
1987 Pan American Games
Indianapolis

BIENVENDIOS. This postcard was created for the Pan Am Games held in Indianapolis. The Indiana State Capitol was explained on the reverse side in English and Spanish.

BALL OR STRIKE? Coach Steve Farley watches pitcher Jon Olson during a scrimmage and calls balls and strikes from behind the hurler. Farley has had six winning seasons and four championships during his 11-year career at Butler . Olson, a sophomore, was the Player of the Year at St. Joseph's High School, Kenosha, Wisconsin.

PRACTICE, PRACTICE, PRACTICE. Assistant Coach Bob Keeney hits balls to infielders during practice in September 2002. Butler's baseball program runs all year now to keep players in shape and ready when the season rolls around in the spring. Other assistants on the team are Jason Taulman and Luke Murphy.

"Tony" Hinkle. Paul "Tony" Hinkle turned the baseball program around and coached the team for 38 seasons in all. The coach and athletic director built the Butler athletic program over half a century. In 1966, the Butler Fieldhouse was renamed in his honor.

RECORD SETTER. Steve Mitchell set the Butler record for longest hitting streak at 24 games in 1977. Steve was also a top pitcher for the Bulldogs and tossed a one-hitter in 1978. He is now a local sports photographer.

SIGN OF THE TIMES. Butler proudly displays a sign showing their latest accomplishments on the ball diamond. The sign sits at Bulldog Park, which is behind Hinkle Fieldhouse, named after Paul "Tony" Hinkle, who coached the program for 32 seasons. The park played host to the 2001 Indiana All-Star games, and several Major League teams hold tryout camps there.

SWING BATTER! An IUPUI player takes a swing at the ball during a game at Victory Field. The Jaguars never had their own baseball field during their playing days from 1979 to 2001. The baseball program was discontinued due to expenses of running the program. The team performed poorly during its existence.

EIGHT
Players from Indianapolis

SOME FORTY major league players can claim Indianapolis as their birthplace. One of the first was a player by the name of Bill Barnes, who played for St. Paul of the Union Association in 1884. Another early player was Toad Ramsey, who played in the American Association in the 1880s. The knuckleball pitcher played for Louisville for five seasons and then St. Louis.

The most famous major league player from Indianapolis is Chuck Klein, who was inducted into the National Baseball Hall of Fame in 1980. The National League outfielder played for four teams in 14 years. He broke National League records in runs scored and extra base hits. He was named MVP in 1932 and appeared in the first All-Star Game the following season.

Several Indianapolis-born players toiled in the Negro Leagues. The most famous was Oscar Charleston, who was inducted into the Hall of Fame in 1976. Another Negro League player was Bill Owens, who played professional ball for eleven years. He got his start with the Indianapolis ABCs then played in the Negro National League for several years.

Other Indianapolis-born major leaguers include Paddy Baumann, Elmer Brown, Rich Coggins, Roy Corthan, Carl Dale, Hooks Dauss, Elmer Duggan, Hod Eller, Jeff James, John Kerins, Ron Keller, Matt Kinzer, Don Leppert, Marshall Locke, Al McCauley, Don Miles, Dennis Musgraves, George Orme, Ray Oyler, Rodney Scott, Joe Slusarski, Ed Summers, Frank Warfield, Bill Whaley, and Jack White, just to name a few.

BRYAN BULLINGTON. The first player selected by the Pittsburgh Pirates in the 2002 Major League Baseball draft was Bullington. The six-foot-five right-handed pitcher earned the selection in the draft after setting several records at Ball State University. Although he was born in Indianapolis, Bullington moved around the state, because his father was a basketball coach. He was graduated from Madison High School and his parents now live in Fishers, an Indianapolis suburb. He would like to get to the majors in a couple of years. "The quicker the better," he explained. However, he was in no hurry to sign with the Pirates as his agent was working out a lucrative contract.

TIM BOGAR. Born in Indianapolis, Bogar moved to Buffalo, Illinois, in his youth. The New York Mets drafted him in 1986 and he broke into the majors with the Mets in 1993. The versatile player became a utility infielder. He was dealt to the Houston Astros and spent several seasons in Houston.

"DONIE BUSH." Owen J. "Donie" Bush was born in Indianapolis and first played in his hometown before going to the majors with the Detroit Tigers in 1908. The following season the shortstop played in the World Series for the Tigers. He played with Detroit until getting traded to the Washington Senators in 1921. His major league career spanned 16 seasons and he hit .261 with nine home runs. The sharp-eyed hitter and speedy runner led the league in walks for five seasons and stole 403 bases during his career.

A.J. ZAPP. Born in Indianapolis and raised in nearby Greenwood, Zapp was drafted in the first round by the Atlanta Braves in 1996. Zapp starred at Center Grove High School earning All-State honors and the Mental Attitude Award. That great attitude helped him survive the injuries and tough times in the minors as he was injured several times. By 2002, the first baseman finally climbed to Triple-A with the Richmond Braves. The promotion allowed him to come back to Indianapolis to play. "It took me a lot longer than I had planned," the power hitting left-hander said.

116

JOHN "RED" CORRIDEN. Seen here talking with his son, who played for Montreal Royals and Brooklyn Dodgers, Corriden played five years in the majors. After his playing career, he returned home to coach with the Indianapolis Indians for two seasons. He also managed the club to a last-place finish in 1930. (Photo courtesy of John Corriden Jr.)

JOE McCABE   Catcher   MINN TWINS

JOE McCABE. McCabe was a most valuable player at Purdue University in 1960 and the second best hitter in the Big 10, but injuries limited his major league career to two years, 1964-65. The Indianapolis native lettered in football, basketball and baseball at Lebanon High School. The Washington Senators signed him after college for $25,000. After two short stints in the majors, he found himself back in the minors. When his Hawaii team came to play in Indianapolis on August 13, 1965, the Indians declared the evening Joe McCabe Night. He broke his finger during the game, which ended his baseball career.

GARY THURMAN. Thurman played six years with Kansas City before going to three other teams during a nine-year career in the majors from 1987-1995. Born in Indianapolis, he was an all-state quarterback and record-setting baseball player at North Central High School. Purdue offered him a football scholarship, but he chose baseball after Kansas City drafted him in the first round in 1983. The outfielder never materialized into an impact player in the majors.

JEFF PARRETT. Parrett was a relief pitcher in the majors for ten years, 1986-96. Born in Indianapolis, Parrett's family moved to Lexington, Kentucky, when he was six months old. He was drafted by the Milwaukee Brewers in 1983, but ended up with Montreal. He played in the minors with Indianapolis before the Expos promoted him to the majors in 1986. Then he went on the frequent flyer program and played for six teams in ten years. His career ended in St. Louis in 1996. Parrett's career record was 56-43, with 22 saves.

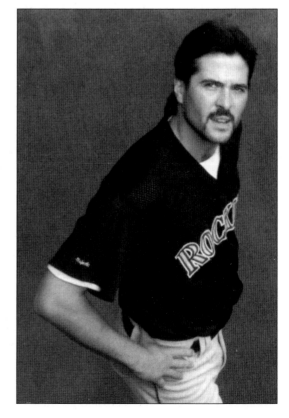

NINE
Vintage Baseball

VINTAGE BASEBALL came to Indianapolis in 1992 when the Freetown Village Ball Team began to play each summer in the Circle City. Like the first teams of African-Americans in the city, the team, which is sponsored by Freetown Village, a living history museum, adopted rules from 1870 to demonstrate the sport of baseball. Back then only underhanded pitching was allowed. The ball was a little softer than today's hardball and nobody used gloves. The gentlemen's game had strict rules against profanity, spitting on the ground, or arguing with the umpire. The team played their games in Fall Creek Park. In 2000, the team took on the Ohio Muffins at a game in Military Park as part of a special event by the Indiana Historical Society. The team didn't play in 2001, but does plan to take the field again in 2003 against the White River Base Ball Team at the same event.

The White River nine was formed in 2001 at Conner Prairie, a living history village, in the suburb of Fishers. The team of volunteers was organized by Dan Freas and started playing against other vintage baseball teams. The White River nine adopted the rules of 1886 to go along with the area of the village they play, the 1886 Liberty Corner. In 2002, the team joined the Vintage Base Ball Association, which was formed in 1996 to organize the sport more throughout the country. The association requires its members to play six games against other vintage teams.

Another vintage team also began play in 2001. The Indianapolis Blues was formed by one of the White River team players, Scott Anderson. The Blues adopted the rules from 1864. They took their name from the 1877 Indianapolis team, which were members of the League Alliance, believed by many to be the first minor league. The 1877 team called themselves the Blues, because their uniforms were that color.

The Blues played just two games in 2001 and beat the White River Base Ball Club on both occasions. In May 2002, the White River team held a Spring Festival at Conner Prairie and hosted the Indianapolis Blues, the Deep River Grinders from Hobart, and the Cincinnati Red Stockings. The White River club also played four other games in 2002 and put on demonstrations in Zionsville and Noblesville. The team now allows visitors to the village to play on the team. The White River team has played a dozen contests against a number of other vintage baseball clubs. The Blues also played about a dozen contests in 2002.

BIG SWING! A ballplayer from Freetown Village takes a mighty swing like Casey at the bat. The ball team uses rules from 1870 when they play. (Photo courtesy of Freetown Village.)

PLAYERS AND CRANKS. The Freetown Village Ball Team brought along cranks as well when they played the Ohio Village Muffins in Columbus, Ohio. (Photo courtesy of Freetown Village.)

FREETOWN VILLAGE. The Freetown Village Ball Team has been playing vintage ball since 1992 in Indianapolis. Freetown Village is a living history museum in Indianapolis. (Photo courtesy of Freetown Village.)

ATTENTION! Members of the White River Base Ball team and Cincinnati Red Stockings line up before taking to the field for a game of vintage base ball in Cincinnati. The Red Stockings use the rules from 1869, which only permitted underhanded pitching. The two teams met twice in 2002 with the Red Stockings winning both contests.

A Hit! A player from the Cincinnati Red Stockings takes a lick at the ball during a game against the White River Base Ball team from Fishers, Indiana. Bunting had yet to be invented in 1869, so players would chop at the ball, which resulted in a bunt-like effect. The hotly contested game was held in late July 2002 and was won by the Red Stockings, 24-22.

Indianapolis Blues. The Indianapolis Blues use a large "I" logo for their uniforms. The original logo was used by the 1877 Indianapolis Blues. The Blues were organized in 2001. (Art by Randi Madden.)

SAXON'S BAND. The pitcher for Saxon's Band lets go of a pitch at the 1886 Liberty Corner field at Conner Prairie. The band performed and played a game of baseball twice at Conner Prairie in 2002. The band comes from Kentucky.

READY FOR ANYTHING. The third baseman for Saxon's Band takes the usual stand in preparation for anything. Band members shed their coats to play baseball between performances at Conner Prairie in 2002. The band played music from the 1800s for the guests at the living history museum.

STRIKE! A young visitor to Conner Prairie takes a swipe at a pitch during a game of vintage base ball. Two members of the White River Base Ball team await the pitch.

SWING BATTER! Paul "Three Finger" Drew gets ready to swing at a pitch during an inter-squad game at Conner Prairie. Drew got his nickname from the famous Indiana hurler, "Three Finger" Brown, a pitcher for the Chicago Cubs. All of the players have nicknames, such as "Thunderbolt," "Scooter," "Dungheap," "Gramps," "Tex," and "Groundhog."

FASTBALL! "Wild Bill" Madden lets go of a pitch during a game against Saxon's Band. The author still likes to play what he writes about—baseball. Madden has written eight books on the subject, including this one.

BASEBALL LESSONS. A member of the White River Base Ball team, Kevin "Knuckles" Cole, gives a lesson on how to hold a bat to a visitor to Conner Prairie. After games are held at the field, the players will allow visitors to participate in a game of vintage base ball.

BIBLIOGRAPHY

Clark, Dick and Larry Lester. *The Negro Leagues Book*. Cleveland, Ohio: Society for American Baseball Research, 1994

DeBono, Paul. *The Indianapolis ABCs, 1997*. Jefferson, North Carolina: McFarland & Company, Inc., Publishers, 1997.

Nemec, David. *The Beer and Whiskey League*. New York: Lyons & Burford, Publishers, 1994.

———. *The Great Encyclopedia of 19th Century Major League Baseball*. New York: Donald I. Fine Books, 1997.

Reddick, David B. and Kim M. Rogers. *The Magic of Indians' Baseball: 1887–1987*. Indianapolis: Indians, Inc., 1988.

Riley, James A. *The Biographical Encyclopedia of the Negro Leagues*. New York: Carroll & Graf Publishers, Inc., 1994.

NEWSPAPERS

Indianapolis Daily Journal
Indianapolis News
Indianapolis Star
The Indianapolis Times